GUIDEBOOK ON INDIAN COPYRIGHT LAW FOR CREATORS AND USERS

ISERDINDIA ANALYTICS

"To all the creators and users of copyrighted works in India, who strive to balance the protection of their rights with the promotion of creativity and innovation. May this guidebook serve as a valuable resource in navigating the complexities of Indian copyright law and help foster a culture of respect for the rights of creators and users alike."

Contents

Foreword

Copyright law is a complex and ever-evolving field that affects everyone from creators and artists to users and consumers. In the digital age, it has become more important than ever for individuals and organizations to have a deep understanding of copyright law and its implications. That is why we are proud to introduce "Guidebook on Indian Copyright Law for Creators and Users," written by the experts at ISERDIndia.

This guidebook is a comprehensive and accessible resource for anyone looking to navigate the Indian copyright landscape. It covers all the key concepts, principles, and practices of Indian copyright law, including the rights of creators, the rights of users, and the various exceptions and limitations that apply. The book also covers the important topic of copyright infringement and the remedies available to rights holders.

One of the most valuable aspects of this guidebook is that it is written specifically for creators and users of copyrighted works in India. Whether you are an artist, musician, writer, or filmmaker, or a user of copyrighted works such as software, books, or films, this guidebook will provide you with the knowledge and tools you need to protect your rights and understand your obligations under Indian copyright law.

ISERDIndia is a well-known organization in the field of Intellectual Property Rights, providing guidance and assistance to creators and users of copyrighted works in India. The organization has a team of experts who have deep knowledge of Indian copyright law and its practical application. The team have put their expertise in this book, providing a valuable resource for anyone interested in understanding Indian copyright law.

We highly recommend "Guidebook on Indian Copyright Law for Creators and Users" to anyone looking for a comprehensive and accessible guide to Indian copyright law. Whether you are a creator, user, or simply someone with an interest in intellectual property rights, this guidebook will be an invaluable resource for you.

Preface

"Welcome to the "Guidebook on Indian Copyright Law for Creators and Users" written by ISERDIndia organization. This guidebook is designed to provide a comprehensive understanding of Indian copyright law for creators and users alike.

Copyright law is an essential tool that protects the rights of creators and ensures that their works are properly acknowledged and compensated. As technology continues to evolve and the ways in which we create and consume content changes, it is more important than ever to have a clear understanding of copyright law. This guidebook aims to provide that understanding by providing a comprehensive overview of Indian copyright law and its various provisions.

This guidebook is written by experts from ISERDIndia organization, who have extensive experience in the field of copyright law. They have made every effort to ensure that the information provided in this guidebook is accurate, up-to-date, and easy to understand. The guidebook covers the major aspects of Indian copyright law, including the rights of creators, the scope of copyright protection, and the remedies available to copyright owners.

This guidebook is intended for creators, users, and anyone else with an interest in copyright law. Whether you are a musician, a writer, a photographer, or a software developer, you will find valuable information in this guidebook. Users of copyrighted works will also find the guidebook useful, as it provides information on what is and is not allowed under copyright law.

We hope that you will find this guidebook to be a valuable resource as you navigate the complexities of Indian copyright law. We wish you all the best in your creative endeavors and look forward to your contributions to the world of art and culture."

Acknowledgements

We are grateful to our team at ISERD India for their invaluable contributions in editing, formatting and publishing the book.

We would also like to extend our thanks to our partners and sponsors for their support in making this publication a reality. Their contributions have been instrumental in bringing this valuable resource to the public.

Finally, we would like to acknowledge the contributions of all the creators and users of copyrighted works. Their efforts have shaped the landscape of Indian Copyright law, and it is our hope that this guidebook will be a useful tool for them in navigating the complexities of copyright law in India.

We hope that this guidebook will be a valuable resource for creators and users of copyrighted works and will help to promote a better understanding of Indian Copyright law.

Thank you.

Prologue

"Welcome to 'Guidebook on Indian Copyright Law for Creators and Users', a comprehensive guide to navigating the complex world of Indian copyright law. This book is designed to help creators and users of copyrighted materials understand their rights and responsibilities under the law, and to provide them with the tools they need to protect and exploit their creations.

This guidebook covers a wide range of topics, including the basics of copyright law, the rights of creators and users, and the legal remedies available to those whose rights have been infringed.

Whether you are a professional artist, musician, writer, or designer, or simply someone who enjoys creating and consuming copyrighted materials, this guidebook is an essential tool for understanding and protecting your rights. We provide you with an in-depth look into the Indian Copyright law and its nuances, as well as practical advice on how to navigate the legal system.

In this guidebook, we will explore the various types of copyrighted works, the rights of creators and users, and the legal remedies available to those whose rights have been infringed. We will also cover the practical aspects of copyright law, such as how to register your work and how to license your creations.

We hope that this guidebook will serve as a valuable resource for creators and users of copyrighted materials, and that it will help you to better understand and protect your rights under Indian copyright law. So, whether you are a professional artist, musician, writer, or designer, or simply someone who enjoys creating and consuming copyrighted materials, this guidebook is an essential tool for understanding and protecting your rights. Let's dive into the world of Indian Copyright Law together!"

CHAPTER I

INTRODUCTION TO COPYRIGHT

If you post photos on Facebook, write emails, post videos on you tube, then you are a copyright holder. If you are playing Arijit Singh songs at your restaurant, without his permission, you are technically a copyright infringer. Copyright is that branch of intellectual property rights which protects artistic, literary, dramatic, musical and the like works. The concept of related rights annexed to copyrights protects sound recordings, cinematograph films and performers.

Copyright is not a single right, it is a bundle of rights. In simplest terms, copyright is the right to copy, but it is not limited to that. It is also the right to perform, to translate, to make adaptations, derivative works etc.

Copyright is a legal concept that grants the creators of original works exclusive rights to control the use and distribution of their creations. This includes literary, dramatic, musical, and artistic works, as well as certain other types of intellectual property, such as sound recordings and films. Copyright law is intended to encourage creativity and innovation by giving creators the ability to control how their works are used and by providing them with financial incentives to create new works.

The concept of copyright dates back to the 16th century, but it has evolved significantly over time, particularly with the advent of new technologies and the digital age. Today, copyright law is governed by international treaties and national laws, which vary from country to country. However, there are certain basic principles that are common to most copyright systems around the world.

One of the most fundamental principles of copyright is the idea of originality. In order for a work to be protected by copyright, it must be original and the creation of the author. This means that the work must be the result of the author's own intellectual effort and must not be copied from someone else. Additionally, the work must be fixed in a tangible form, such as on paper, in a digital file, or as a recording.

Once a work is protected by copyright, the copyright owner has the exclusive right to reproduce, distribute, and display the work publicly, as well as to create derivative works based on the original. This means that others cannot use the work without the permission of the copyright owner, unless they fall under the exception of fair use or the copyright has expired.

Another important principle of copyright is the idea of duration. Copyright protection lasts for a certain period of time, after which the work enters the public domain and can be used freely by anyone. The duration of copyright protection varies depending on the type of work and the country in which it was created. However, in most countries, copyright protection lasts for the life of the author plus a certain number of years after the author's death.

Copyright law also includes certain exceptions, such as fair use and the doctrine of first sale, which allow certain limited uses of copyrighted works without the permission of the copyright owner. Fair use is an exception to the exclusive rights of copyright owners, which allows for the use of copyrighted material for certain purposes, such as criticism, news reporting, teaching, scholarship, or research. The doctrine of first sale, on the other hand, allows the owner of a legally acquired copy of a work to sell or otherwise dispose of that copy without the permission of the copyright owner.

In conclusion, Copyright is a legal concept that grants creators of original works exclusive rights to control the use and distribution of their creations, it encourages creativity and innovation by giving creators the ability to control how their works are used and by providing them with financial incentives to create new works. Copyright law is governed by international treaties and national laws, which vary from country to country, but there are certain basic principles that are common to most copyright systems around the world.

Few examples of how copyright applies in different situations:

1. **A novel:** An author writes a novel and publishes it. The author holds the copyright to the novel and has the exclusive right to reproduce it, distribute copies of it, and publicly display or perform it. This means that others cannot legally copy or distribute the novel without the author's permission.

2. **A song:** A musician writes and records a song. The musician holds the copyright to the song and has the exclusive right to reproduce it, distribute copies of it, and publicly perform it. This means that others cannot legally make copies of the song or perform it without the musician's permission.

3. **A photograph:** A photographer takes a photograph and sells it to a magazine. The photographer holds the copyright to the photograph and has the exclusive right to reproduce it, distribute copies of it, and publicly display it. This means that the magazine cannot use the photograph for any other purpose without the photographer's permission.

4. **A movie:** A film studio produces a movie and releases it in theaters. The studio holds the copyright to the movie and has the exclusive right to reproduce it, distribute copies of it, and publicly display or perform it. This means that others cannot legally make copies of the movie or show it without the studio's permission.

5. **A software:** A software developer creates a computer program and sells it. The developer holds the copyright to the software and has the exclusive right to reproduce it, distribute copies of it, and publicly display or perform it. This means that others cannot legally make copies of the software or use it without the developer's permission.

These are just a few examples of how copyright applies to different types of works. It is important to note that there are also exceptions and limitations to copyright protection such as fair use, which allows for the use of copyrighted material in certain situations, such as criticism, commentary, news reporting, and teaching.

CHAPTER II

NEED OF COPYRIGHT

Copyright is important for several reasons, including:

1. **Encouraging creativity:** Copyright provides creators with the incentive to create and share their work by giving them the exclusive right to control how their work is used and by whom. This allows creators to earn a living from their work and to continue to create new works.
2. **Protecting property rights:** Copyright gives creators the legal means to protect their work from unauthorized use. This allows creators to control how their work is used and to prevent others from profiting from their work without their permission.
3. **Promoting cultural diversity:** Copyright helps to preserve and promote the diversity of cultural expressions by giving creators the exclusive right to control how their work is used. This allows creators to share their unique perspectives and experiences with the world.
4. **Promoting education and research:** Copyright includes exceptions and limitations, such as fair use, which allows for the use of copyrighted material in certain situations, such as criticism, commentary, news reporting, and teaching. This helps to promote education and research by allowing scholars, educators, and researchers to use copyrighted works in their work.
5. **Encouraging innovation:** Copyright gives creators the exclusive right to control how their work is used. This allows creators to license their work to others, who can then use it to create new works. This helps to promote innovation by allowing new works to be created from existing works.

Overall, copyright provides a balance between protecting creators' rights and allowing for the use of copyrighted material for the benefit of society.

CHAPTER III

RIGHTS OF A COPYRIGHT HOLDER

The rights of a copyright holder include the exclusive right to:

1. **Reproduce the work:** This includes the right to make copies of the work, such as printing books or making copies of a song.
2. **Distribute the work:** This includes the right to sell, rent, or otherwise distribute copies of the work.
3. **Display the work publicly:** This includes the right to show the work in public places, such as displaying a painting in a gallery or showing a movie in a theater.
4. **Perform the work publicly:** This includes the right to perform a work, such as a play or a song, in public places.
5. **Make derivative works:** This includes the right to create new works based on the original work, such as creating a movie adaptation of a novel or creating a new arrangement of a song.
6. **License or assign the rights:** The copyright holder has the right to license or assign any or all of these rights to others, such as allowing a publisher to distribute copies of a book or allowing a film studio to make a movie adaptation of a novel.

The Indian Copyright Act, 1957 recognizes two types of rights for copyright holders: economic rights and moral rights.

Economic rights: Economic rights give the copyright holder the exclusive right to control the use and exploitation of the copyrighted work for commercial gain. This includes the right to reproduce the work, distribute copies of the work, and perform the work in public. The copyright holder has the right to license or assign these economic rights to others, such as allowing a publisher to distribute copies of a book or allowing a film studio to make a movie adaptation of a novel.

Economic rights, also known as exclusive rights, are the rights that are granted to the copyright owner of a work to monetarily benefit from their work. These rights include the ability to reproduce, sell, license, perform, or broadcast the work, among other activities that may generate financial gain for the copyright holder. These rights are transferable, meaning they can be sold, assigned, or licensed for a fixed sum or for royalties. For example, a singer may assign the copyright in their song to a music label, which may further advertise and sell the song, and the singer might receive a single one-time payment for it.

As copyright subsists in original works such as literary, dramatic, musical, cinematographic film, and sound recordings, the authors of these works enjoy economic rights under Section 14 of the Copyright Act.

In regards to literary, dramatic, and musical works, these rights include the ability to reproduce the work into any material form, store the work in any electronic form, issue copies of the work, communicate the work in public, make any sound or cinematographic film about the work, and convert the work in any translation or adaptation. In respect of computer programs, the authors enjoy the right to sell or offer for sale, give on hire or hire any copy of the computer program.

In the case of cinematographic films and film recordings, these rights include the ability to make copies, sell or give on hire any copy, and communicate the work in public. In summary, Economic rights enable the copyright holder to financially benefit from their work, by allowing them to reproduce, sell, license, perform, or broadcast the work, among other activities that generate financial gain for the copyright holder.

Moral rights: Moral rights are a key component of copyright law that recognize the personal connection an author has to their work and their interest in protecting the work's integrity and reputation. These rights are not transferable and remain with the author even after they have transferred their economic rights to another party.

Moral rights consist of two key rights: the right to attribution and the right to integrity. The right to attribution refers to the author's right to be recognized as the creator of a work, and the right to integrity refers to the author's right to protect the work from distortion, mutilation, or other actions that may harm its reputation.

It is important to note that moral rights are personal to the author and can only be transferred upon their death. For example, in the scenario of a singer assigning their economic rights in a song to a music label, they would still retain the right to be recognized as the singer of the song and the right to prevent others from altering the lyrics.

According to Section 57 of the Copyright Act, the two moral rights of the author are the Right of Paternity, which enables an author to claim authorship of the work and prevent others from doing so, and the Right of

Integrity, which empowers the author to prevent any actions that may harm the reputation of the work.

CHAPTER IV

COPYRIGHT SOCIETIES IN INDIA

Copyright societies in India play a crucial role in protecting and managing the rights of copyright holders in the country. These societies are established for specific categories of works, such as musical works, sound recordings, reprographic works, and performers' rights. Some of the notable copyright societies in India include:

- The Indian Performing Right Society Limited (IPRS), which manages the rights of musical works. They can be accessed at www.iprs.org.
- Phonographic Performance Limited (PPL) is a society that manages the rights of sound recordings. However, it has ceased to be Copyright society now.
- Indian Reprographic Rights Organization (IRRO) manages the rights of reprographic works and can be accessed at www.irro.in.
- Indian Singers Rights Association (ISRA) manages the rights of performers and can be accessed at www.isracopyright.com.
- Screenwriters Rights Association of India ("SRAI") is a society that manages the rights of screenwriters
- Society for Copyright Regulations of Indian Producers of Films and Television (SCRIPT) is a society that manages the rights of Producers of Films and Television.

In addition to these copyright societies, there are also other entities that are involved in managing copyright in India, such as the Copyright Office, the Copyright Board, and the Intellectual Property Appellate Board. These entities have different roles and responsibilities in the administration and enforcement of copyright laws in India.

CHAPTER V

THE IDEA EXPRESSION DICHOTOMY

The concept of the idea-expression dichotomy is an important aspect of copyright law, as it helps to distinguish between what is protected by copyright and what is not. While one may have a number of ideas, the law of copyright does not protect these ideas per se, but rather the expression of those ideas.

For example, if an individual has a storyline in mind where two people from different backgrounds fall in love, and their families oppose the relationship, ultimately leading to the couple's separation and suicide, the copyright does not exist on this idea of a story. However, if an individual were to create a movie with this storyline, that movie would be protected by copyright.

Similarly, if an individual has an idea to paint a sunset in the mountains with pink sky, anyone can use this idea, but the individual's painting would be protected by copyright. It is important to understand that copyright only protects specific expressions and not the facts or ideas conveyed by that expression. This allows different authors and artists to convey the same idea in their own manner and style, creating a variety of versions for audiences to choose from.

It's worth noting that ideas for patentable works are protected under the patent laws, but not by copyright laws. However, ideas can be protected under the law of unfair competition, which implies that the second party is free riding on the labor and investment of the first In summary, the idea-expression dichotomy plays a crucial role in copyright law, as it allows for a balance between protecting the rights of creators and allowing for further creative expression and innovation.

CHAPTER VI

PROCEDURE OF COPYRIGHT REGISTRATION IN INDIA

The Indian Copyright Act, 1957 and the Copyright Rules, 2013 outline the procedure for registering copyrights in India. According to Chapter X of the Indian Copyright Act and Rule 70 of the Copyright Rules, the following steps should be taken to register a copyright:

1. Application: The author or applicant can file an application for copyright registration themselves or through an authorized legal representative. The application can be made in person at the copyright office, via speed/registered post, or through the e-filing facility available on the official website of the Copyrights Office (copyright.gov.in). Each application, in Form IV, must be accompanied by the appropriate fee as prescribed in the second schedule of the Rules. Fees range from 500 INR to 40,000 INR, depending on the form of work. The fee can be paid through a Demand Draft or Indian Postal Order made payable to the "Registrar of Copyright Payable at New Delhi" or through e-payment. The application must include the following information:

a) Name, address, and nationality of the applicant;

b) Nature of the applicant's interest in the work;

c) Title of the work;

d) Name, address, and nationality of the author of the work, and if the author is deceased, the date of their death;

e) Language of the work;

f) Whether the work is published or unpublished;

g) Year and country of first publication and name, address, and nationality of the publisher;

h) Year and countries of subsequent publications, if any, and name, address, and nationality of subsequent publishers;

i) Name, address, and nationality of a person authorized to assign or license the rights comprising the copyright, if any;

j) A no-objection certificate signed by the author (if different from the applicant);

k) A Vakalatnama or Power of attorney signed by the advocate and the party (if the application is made by the advocate of the party);

l) Three copies of the published work must be sent along with the application.

m) Application for registration of a computer program must be filed with the source and object code.

n) Application for registration of an artistic work used or capable of being used in relation to goods must be filed with a statement to that effect and a no-objection certificate from the Registrar of Trademarks.

o) Application for registration of an artistic work capable of being registered as a design must be filed with a statement in the form of an affidavit stating that it has not been registered under the Designs Act, 2000 and has not been applied to any article through an industrial process.

p) The application must be signed by the applicant or the advocate;

q) The applicant must provide their mobile number and email address to receive the filing number.

2. Examination: Upon filing the application, the applicant will receive a diary number. There is a mandatory wait period of 30 days for the filing of "No Objection" against the author's claim. If an objection is filed against the copyright claim, it may take an additional month for the Registrar of Copyrights to provide both parties with an opportunity to hear the matter. After the decision on the ownership or if the objection is rejected, the application will be scrutinized. The applicant will be given 30 days to remove any discrepancies found during the examination process.

3. Registration: Upon submission of the necessary documents and if the Copyright Registrar is satisfied with the completeness and correctness of the claim made in the application, the Registrar will enter the details of the copyright in the Register of Copyrights and issue a Certificate of Registration

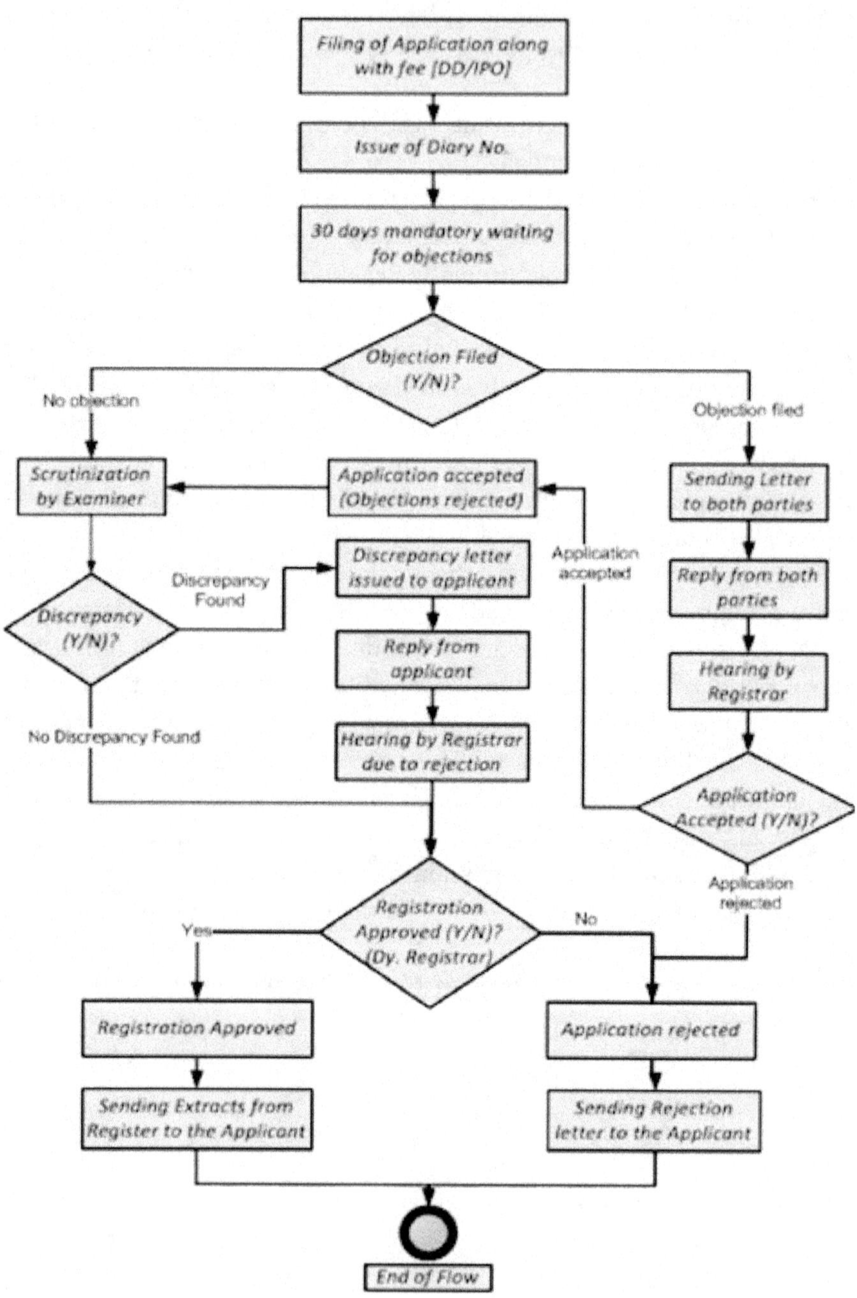

Copyright Registration Process in India

13

CHAPTER VII

TERM OF COPYRIGHT

Section 22 to 29 of the Copyright Act, 1957 lays out the terms of copyright protection for various types of works. In general, copyright lasts for a period of 60 years. Specifically, the terms are as follows:

- For literary, dramatic, musical, or artistic works, the copyright term is the lifetime of the author plus 60 years following the author's death.
- For anonymous and pseudonymous works, the copyright term is 60 years from the date of first publication.
- For works of public undertakings and government works, the copyright term is 60 years from the date of first publication.
- For works of international organizations, the copyright term is 60 years from the date of first publication.
- For sound recordings, the copyright term is 60 years from the date of publication.
- For cinematographic films, the copyright term is 60 years from the date of publication.

CHAPTER VIII

COPYRIGHT INFRINGEMENT

The Copyright Act, 1957 grants the holder of a copyright exclusive rights to utilize and commercially exploit their work in any manner they see fit. Infringement of copyright occurs when a person engages in unauthorized use of a copyrighted work, such as reproducing, displaying, performing, or distributing the work without the permission of the right holder. Any actions that impinge upon the exclusive rights of a right holder and undermine such rights would be considered an act of infringement. Even if there is no commercial exploitation of the author's work, it would still constitute infringement, unless it falls under an exception specified in the act.

Infringement can take two forms: primary infringement and secondary infringement. Primary infringement refers to direct infringement of a copyright holder's exclusive rights, while secondary infringement refers to the act of offering or providing infringing copies or devices to the public.

1. Primary Infringement: Section 51(a) of the Copyright Act, 1957 addresses primary infringement, which encompasses the unauthorized reproduction or duplication of a copyrighted work. This type of infringement involves direct interference with the exclusive rights of the copyright holder, as outlined in the act. Specifically, primary infringement may occur through the following actions:

- Engaging in any activity for which a license is required, but has not been obtained, as specified in the act.
- Allowing a place of profit to be used for communicating the work to the public without a license, if such communication constitutes an infringement of the copyright.

2. Secondary Infringement: Secondary infringement, as per Section 51(b) of the Indian Copyright Act, 1957, refers to acts that do not involve direct copying of a copyrighted work, but still constitute infringement of the copyright holder's exclusive rights. The following actions are considered as secondary infringement:

- The manufacture, sale, or rental of a copyrighted work without permission from the copyright holder.
- The distribution of a copyrighted work, whether for commercial gain or in a quantity that harms the copyright holder's interests, without a license or permission.
- The public display or trade of a copyrighted work without permission.
- The importation into India of copyrighted works without permission from the copyright holder.

Overall, these acts are considered secondary infringement as they involve the distribution, sale, or commercialization of copyrighted works without the permission of the copyright holder.

Some examples of copyright infringement include:

- Reproducing a copyrighted book, music album, or film without permission from the copyright holder.
- Distributing a copyrighted work, such as a song or movie, on the internet without permission.
- Selling counterfeit copies of a copyrighted work, such as designer clothing or handbags.
- Using a copyrighted image or logo on a website or in advertising without permission from the copyright holder.
- Publicly performing a copyrighted song or play without obtaining a license to do so.
- Reproducing or distributing a copyrighted software program without permission from the copyright holder.
- Creating a derivative work, such as a translation or adaptation, without permission from the copyright holder.
- Recording a copyrighted music performance and selling or distributing the recording without permission.

It's worth noting that there are some exceptions like fair use, fair dealing, and some other exceptions which are defined under the copyright act,1957. It's also important to seek legal advice before using copyrighted material in case of any doubts.

How to determine infringement?

The determination of copyright infringement can be a complex and subjective process, as artistic creations can vary greatly in terms of originality and similarity. To determine whether a particular work has been copied from an existing work, various tests can be applied. One such test is the "substantial similarity" test, which examines whether the alleged copy contains elements that are substantially similar to the copyrighted work. However, even if substantial similarity is found, the presence of a "qualitative element" that transforms the work into a new creation may negate the claim of infringement.

Another test is the "test of personality" which assesses how much personal effort has been put into the creation of a work to determine if it was created independently or copied. Additionally, the "economic test" evaluates infringement by examining the demand placed on the original work, and the "extrinsic" and "intrinsic" tests utilize expert and non-expert testimony respectively to assess similarity between two works. Ultimately, it is important to consider the essence of the work and determine if it has been breached by the alleged infringement.

Innocent infringement

In the realm of copyright infringement, the concept of "innocent infringement" refers to instances where an individual creates a work that is substantially similar to an existing copyrighted work, without any intention or knowledge of copying said work. While it may be difficult to establish intent in such cases, it is important to note that the defense of innocent infringement is not a valid defense in copyright infringement matters. This is because allowing such a defense would provide an excuse for individuals to escape liability for infringement. However, it is worth noting that in certain cases, an individual's status as an innocent infringer may be considered as a mitigating factor when determining damages in an infringement case.

Exceptions to infringement

The Copyright Act recognizes certain exceptions and limitations to the exclusive rights of the copyright holder. These exceptions have been established to balance the public interest with the private interest of the copyright holder. As per Article 13 of the TRIPS Agreement, member countries are allowed to implement exceptions to copyright infringement, provided that they adhere to the three-step test.

This test states that exceptions must be limited to specific cases, should not conflict with the normal exploitation of the copyrighted work, and should not unreasonably prejudice the legitimate interests of the right holder.

Different jurisdictions provide for different exceptions to copyright infringement, which must comply with Article 13 of the TRIPS Agreement. These exceptions can be broadly classified into three categories: Fair Use, Fair Dealing, and Permitted Acts. These exceptions are designed to balance the interest of copyright holders with the public interest in the use and dissemination of copyrighted works.

Section 52 of the Indian Copyright Act of 1957 lists several exceptions to copyright infringement. These exceptions are designed to allow for certain types of use of copyrighted works without the permission of the copyright owner, in order to promote the public interest and the free flow of information.

The exceptions to copyright infringement listed in Section 52 of the Indian Copyright Act include:

- **Fair dealing:** This exception allows for the use of copyrighted works for the purpose of criticism, review, news reporting, teaching, scholarship, or research, as long as the use is fair and not for commercial purposes.
- **Reproduction by a library or archive:** This exception allows libraries and archives to reproduce copyrighted works for the purpose of preservation, research, or study.
- **Reproduction of a work by a broadcasting organization:** This exception allows broadcasting organizations to reproduce copyrighted works for the purpose of broadcasting them.
- **Incidental inclusion of a work in an artistic work, sound recording, cinematograph film, or broadcast:** This exception allows for the incidental inclusion of a copyrighted work in another work, such as a film or television show, without infringing on the copyright.
- **Time-shifting:** This exception allows for the recording of a broadcast for the purpose of watching it at a later time, as long as the recording is for personal use and not for commercial purposes.
- **Public exhibition of a work by an educational institution or organization:** This exception allows educational institutions and organizations to exhibit copyrighted works for the purpose of instruction.
- **Use of a work for the purpose of a judicial proceeding or for the giving of professional advice:** This exception allows for the use of copyrighted works in a judicial proceeding or for the purpose of giving professional advice.

- **Certain use of a computer program:** This exception allows for the use of a computer program in certain situations, such as reverse engineering or interoperability, as long as the use is not for commercial purposes.

It is important to note that the above exceptions are subject to certain conditions and limitations and not all uses that fall under these exceptions are permissible, if not done in a fair manner. Furthermore, the courts have the power to decide whether a particular use falls under the scope of these exceptions or not.

In summary, Section 52 of the Indian Copyright Act of 1957 lists several exceptions to copyright infringement, including fair dealing, reproduction by a library or archive, reproduction of a work by a broadcasting organization, incidental inclusion of a work in an artistic work, time-shifting, public exhibition of a work by an educational institution or organization, use of a work for the purpose of a judicial proceeding or for the giving of professional advice, and certain use of a computer program. These exceptions are designed to allow for certain types of use of copyrighted works without the permission of the copyright owner, in order to promote the public interest and the free flow of information. However, these exceptions are subject to certain conditions and limitations and not all uses that fall under these exceptions are permissible.

Remedies of Copyright Infrigement

Section 55 of the Indian Copyright Act of 1957 outlines the remedies for copyright infringement under Indian law. These remedies include both civil and criminal remedies, and are intended to provide copyright owners with the means to protect their rights and seek redress for any infringement that occurs.

Some of the remedies for copyright infringement according to Section 55 of Indian Copyright Act are:

- **Injunctions:** A court may issue an injunction ordering the infringing party to stop using the copyrighted work, or to prevent the infringing party from using the work in the future. This is a common remedy in civil lawsuits for copyright infringement.
- **Damages:** A court may award damages to the copyright owner for any loss or injury suffered as a result of the infringement. This can include lost profits, as well as any other losses or harm caused by the infringement.

- **Account of Profits:** A court may order the infringing party to account for any profits made as a result of the infringement, and to pay those profits to the copyright owner. This remedy is intended to prevent the infringing party from benefiting financially from the infringement.
- **Delivery-up or destruction of infringing copies:** A court may order the infringing party to deliver up or destroy any infringing copies of the copyrighted work. This remedy is intended to prevent the infringing party from continuing to use or distribute the infringing copies.
- **Criminal Remedies:** Criminal remedies for copyright infringement may include imprisonment and fines. Criminal remedies may be sought in cases where the infringement is done with the intention to make a profit or commercial gain.

It is important to note that the remedies available under the Indian Copyright Act are not mutually exclusive and the court has the discretion to award one or more remedies as per the circumstances of the case. Additionally, the copyright owner must prove the infringement in order to claim the remedies.

In summary, Section 55 of the Indian Copyright Act of 1957 outlines several remedies for copyright infringement, including injunctions, damages, account of profits, delivery-up or destruction of infringing copies, and criminal remedies such as imprisonment and fines. These remedies are intended to provide copyright owners with the means to protect their rights and seek redress for any infringement that occurs. The remedies available under the Indian Copyright Act are not mutually exclusive and the court has the discretion to award one or more remedies as per the circumstances of the case.

Section 63 and 63A of the Indian Copyright Act of 1957 outline the penalties for copyright infringement under Indian law. These penalties are intended to deter and punish individuals and entities who engage in copyright infringement.

Section 63 of the Indian Copyright Act of 1957 provides for imprisonment and fines for copyright infringement. The penalties under this section are as follows:

- For the first offence of infringement, the offender can be imprisoned for a term of up to six months, or be fined up to Rs. 50,000, or both.

- For a second or subsequent offence of infringement, the offender can be imprisoned for a term of up to three years, or be fined up to Rs. 200,000, or both.

Section 63A of the Indian Copyright Act of 1957 provides for enhanced penalties for commercial infringement of copyright. The penalties under this section are as follows:

- For commercial infringement of copyright, the offender can be imprisoned for a term of up to three years, or be fined up to Rs. 2,00,000, or both.
- For subsequent offence of commercial infringement of copyright, the offender can be imprisoned for a term of up to six years and also be fined up to Rs. 3,00,000.

It's important to note that under the Indian Copyright Act, any person who knowingly infringes or abets the infringement of copyright, can be held liable for penalties, and it's not limited to only the person who is responsible for the actual infringement.

Additionally, in case of commercial infringement of copyright, it is not necessary for the prosecution to prove knowledge or intention to infringe copyright, the liability would lie on the person who carried out the commercial infringement.

In summary, Section 63 and 63A of the Indian Copyright Act of 1957 provides for penalties for copyright infringement. Section 63 provides for imprisonment and fines for copyright infringement, while Section 63A provides for enhanced penalties for commercial infringement of copyright, which includes imprisonment and fines. These penalties are intended to deter and punish individuals and entities who engage in copyright infringement. The Indian Copyright Act holds any person who knowingly infringes or abets the infringement of copyright liable for penalties, and it's not limited to only the person who is responsible for the actual infringement. Additionally, in case of commercial infringement of copyright, it is not necessary for the prosecution to prove knowledge or intention to infringe copyright, the liability would lie on the person who carried out the commercial infringement.

Controlling Infringement at Borders

The Indian Customs Act, 1962 and the Intellectual Property Rights (Imported Goods) Enforcement Rules, 2007 are the main laws in India that deal with controlling infringement at borders. These laws provide the framework for the Indian government to prevent the import of goods that infringe on copyright and other intellectual property rights.

The Indian Customs Act, 1962 empowers the Customs authorities to seize goods suspected of infringing copyright, trademark, or other intellectual property rights at the border. This is done by providing a mechanism for the rights holder to register their rights with the Customs authorities and to provide them with information on how to identify infringing goods. Once the rights holder has registered their rights, the Customs authorities can detain any goods that they suspect of infringing those rights.

The Intellectual Property Rights (Imported Goods) Enforcement Rules, 2007 (the "Imported Goods Rules") provide the detailed procedure to be followed by the Customs authorities for the enforcement of intellectual property rights at the border. These rules set out the process for rights holders to register their rights with the Customs authorities and for the detention and disposal of infringing goods. The Imported Goods Rules also provide for the appointment of a "Copyright and Trade Mark Agent" to assist the Customs authorities in the identification of infringing goods.

Under the Imported Goods Rules, the rights holder can file an application with the Customs authorities for the registration of their rights. Once the rights are registered, the Customs authorities can detain any goods that they suspect of infringing those rights. The rights holder will then be notified of the detention and given an opportunity to prove that the goods are infringing. If the rights holder is able to prove that the goods are infringing, the Customs authorities will seize the goods and take appropriate action, such as destroying the infringing goods.

In conclusion, the Indian Customs Act, 1962 and the Intellectual Property Rights (Imported Goods) Enforcement Rules, 2007 provide the legal framework for the Indian government to prevent the import of goods that infringe on copyright and other intellectual property rights. These laws empower the Customs authorities to seize goods suspected of infringing copyright, trademark, or other intellectual property rights at the border by providing a mechanism for the rights holder to register their rights with the Customs authorities and to provide them with information on how to identify infringing goods.

CHAPTER IX

FAIR USE IN COPYRIGHT LAW

Fair use is a legal doctrine that allows for the limited use of copyrighted material without obtaining permission from the copyright holder. The concept of fair use is recognized in many jurisdictions, including the United States, and is intended to balance the rights of the copyright holder with the public's interest in the dissemination of information and ideas. In this chapter, we will explore the concept of fair use, the factors that are considered when determining whether a use is fair, and examples of fair use in practice.

The principle of fair use is rooted in the idea that certain uses of copyrighted material should be allowed without permission from the copyright holder in order to promote the public interest. These uses include criticism, commentary, news reporting, teaching, scholarship, and research. Fair use is not an infringement of copyright and is not subject to the payment of royalties.

When determining whether a use is fair, courts consider four main factors:

- The purpose and character of the use, including whether such use is of a commercial nature or is for nonprofit educational purposes
- The nature of the copyrighted work
- The amount and substantiality of the portion used in relation to the copyrighted work as a whole
- The effect of the use upon the potential market for or value of the copyrighted work.

The first factor, the purpose and character of the use, is often considered the most important. If the use is for nonprofit educational or research purposes, it is more likely to be considered fair. If the use is for commercial gain, it is less likely to be considered fair.

The second factor, the nature of the copyrighted work, is also important. If the copyrighted work is creative in nature (such as a novel or a painting), it is less likely to be considered fair use than if the copyrighted work is factual in nature (such as a news article or a scientific study).

The third factor, the amount and substantiality of the portion used in relation to the copyrighted work as a whole, is also important. If the portion used is small in relation to the copyrighted work as a whole, it is more likely to be considered fair use. If the portion used is large in relation to the copyrighted work as a whole, it is less likely to be considered fair use.

The fourth factor, the effect of the use upon the potential market for or value of the copyrighted work, is also important. If the use does not harm the potential market for or value of the copyrighted work, it is more likely to be considered fair use. If the use harms the potential market for or value of the copyrighted work, it is less likely to be considered fair use.

It's important to note that fair use is determined on a case-by-case basis, and the outcome may vary depending on the specific circumstances of the use. Some examples of fair use in practice include:

- Quoting a small portion of a copyrighted work in a book review
- Using a copyrighted image in a news report
- Using a copyrighted song in a parody video
- Reproducing a copyrighted work for the purpose of creating a new work (such as a remix or a mashup)

In conclusion, fair use is a legal doctrine that allows for the limited use of copyrighted material without obtaining permission from the copyright holder. The concept of fair use is intended to balance the rights of the copyright holder with the public's interest in the dissemination of information and ideas. When determining whether a use is fair, courts consider four main factors: the purpose and character of the use, the nature of the copyrighted work, the amount and substantiality of the portion used in relation to the copyrighted work as a whole, and the effect of the use upon.

CHAPTER X

ASSIGNMENT OF COPYRIGHT

Section 18 of the Copyright Act, 1957 governs the assignment of copyrights. The owner of the copyright in an existing work or the prospective owner of the copyright in a future work may assign any portion of the copyright to any person, either wholly or partially. This assignment can be made with or without limitations and can be for the entire term of the copyright or for a specific period of time. The assignment can be made verbally or in writing, through an assignment deed. If the assignment deed is silent on the duration of the assignment, it will be assumed to be for a period of five years. The territorial extent of the assignment will also be assumed to be within India, unless otherwise specified in the assignment.

The assignment must be made in writing, and signed by the assignor or their authorized agent. The assignment should clearly identify the work, specify the rights assigned, and indicate the duration and territorial extent of the assignment. It should also specify the amount of royalty payable to the author or their legal heirs, if any. The assignment may be subject to revision, extension, or termination on terms mutually agreed upon by the parties.

If the assignee fails to exercise the rights assigned to them within a period of one year from the date of the assignment, the assignment will be deemed to have lapsed, unless otherwise specified in the assignment. In the absence of any specific duration or territorial extent stated in the assignment, it will be assumed to be for a period of five years and within India, respectively.

Difference between Assignment and Licensing

Assignment and licensing are two different ways in which a copyright owner can transfer their rights to use a copyrighted work to someone else. Both assignment and licensing are recognized under the Indian Copyright Act of 1957, and both allow the copyright owner to retain the copyright, but they differ in the way the rights are transferred and the level of control the copyright owner retains over the use of the copyrighted work.

Assignment is the transfer of the entire copyright in a work from one person to another. This means that the person to whom the copyright is assigned (the assignee) acquires all the rights of the copyright owner and can use the copyrighted work as they see fit, without the need for further permission from the original copyright owner. Once a copyright is assigned, the original copyright owner no longer has any rights to the work and cannot use or license it without the permission of the assignee.

Licensing, on the other hand, is the permission granted by a copyright owner to use their copyrighted work in a specific way and under certain conditions. The person to whom the license is granted (the licensee) does not acquire any ownership rights in the copyrighted work, but they are granted the right to use the work in a specific way and under specific conditions, such as for a certain period of time or in a specific territory. The copyright owner retains control over the use of the copyrighted work and can revoke the license or grant additional licenses to others.

In summary, the main difference between assignment and licensing according to Indian Copyright Law is that assignment transfers the entire copyright to the assignee, while licensing grants permission to use the copyrighted work in a specific way and under certain conditions. In assignment, the original copyright owner loses all rights to the work, while in licensing, the copyright owner retains control over the use of the copyrighted work and can revoke the license or grant additional licenses to others.

CHAPTER XI

DOCTRINE OF FIRST SALE

The doctrine of first sale, also known as the exhaustion of rights doctrine, is a principle in copyright law that allows the owner of a legally acquired copy of a work to sell or otherwise dispose of that copy without the permission of the copyright owner. This means that once a copyright owner has sold a copy of their work, they no longer have the exclusive right to control the distribution of that particular copy.

In India, the doctrine of first sale is recognized under the Indian Copyright Act of 1957. Section 14 of the Act states that the copyright owner's exclusive right to distribute their work "shall be deemed to be exhausted in respect of any particular copy" once that copy has been sold with the copyright owner's permission. This means that the person who buys a copy of a copyrighted work can resell it, lend it, or give it away without infringing on the copyright owner's rights. However, it should be noted that the right to reproduce the work is not exhausted by the first sale and still stays with the copyright owner.

This principle applies to all types of copyrighted works, including books, films, music, and software. It is important to note that the doctrine of first sale applies only to the distribution of physical copies of a work and not to digital copies.

This principle allows the market to function smoothly, it encourages the distribution and sale of copyrighted works, and also allows the owners of the legally purchased copies to dispose them as per their wish.

In summary, the doctrine of first sale, also known as the exhaustion of rights doctrine, is a principle in Indian Copyright Law that allows the owner of a legally acquired copy of a work to sell or otherwise dispose of that copy without the permission of the copyright owner. It applies to all types of copyrighted works and is recognized under the Indian Copyright Act of 1957.

CHAPTER XII

POWERPOINT AND COPYRIGHT

The use of images from printed material in PowerPoint presentations is permissible, provided that the usage adheres to copyright laws and regulations. It is important to note that reproducing diagrams, charts, and other visual elements from printed materials for purposes other than teaching or research may require obtaining permission from the copyright owner, who may not necessarily be the author of the article.

In regards to the use of clips from YouTube in PowerPoint presentations, it is acceptable to link to and play a clip in a lecture as long as the original clip was published online by the legitimate copyright owner. However, it is important to note that copying the clip or recording the lecture while the clip is playing may be a violation of copyright laws. Additionally, embedding the YouTube widget into the PowerPoint and placing the PPT in an online platform such as Moodle for student access is permissible.

Quotations can also be used in PowerPoint presentations, provided that they are properly acknowledged and cited in accordance with copyright laws and regulations. It is important to give credit to the original author and source of the quote.

CHAPTER XIII

CASE LAWS

R.G. Anand v. Delux Films AIR 1978 SC 1613:

Facts: R.G. Anand, a well-known scriptwriter, filed a suit against Delux Films for copyright infringement of his script for the film "Haathi Mere Saathi." Anand alleged that the defendants had copied his script and made the film without his permission or authorization.

Issue: The main issue in this case was whether Delux Films had infringed upon Anand's copyright by copying his script for the film "Haathi Mere Saathi."

Judgement: The Supreme Court of India held that Delux Films had indeed infringed upon Anand's copyright by copying his script for the film "Haathi Mere Saathi." The court noted that there were striking similarities between the two scripts and that Delux Films had not provided any evidence of independent creation. As a result, the court ordered Delux Films to pay Anand damages and to deliver up all infringing copies of the film to him. The court also granted a permanent injunction against Delux Films, preventing them from reproducing the infringing script in any form. This landmark judgement established that copyright infringement can be proved by showing similarities between two works and the burden of proof of independent creation of the infringing work lies on the defendant.

Mysore Sales International Ltd. v. The Indian Performing Right Society Limited (IPRS) AIR 2007 SC 868:

Facts: In this case, the Indian Performing Right Society Limited (IPRS) had granted a license to Mysore Sales International Ltd. (MSIL) to perform copyrighted songs. However, the parties had a dispute over the royalty fees to be paid by MSIL to IPRS. MSIL argued that they should only have to pay a minimal amount, while IPRS argued that MSIL should pay a higher amount based on the terms of the license agreement.

Issue: The main issue in this case was whether MSIL was required to pay the higher royalty fees as claimed by IPRS, or whether they were only required to pay a minimal amount as argued by MSIL.

Judgment: The Supreme Court of India ruled in favor of IPRS, stating that MSIL was required to pay the higher royalty fees as per the terms of the license agreement. The Court held that the license agreement was valid and binding and that MSIL was obliged to pay the royalties as per the agreement. The Court also held that IPRS was entitled to enforce the agreement and claim the royalties due to them. The court also held that the agreement is valid and binding and IPRS is entitled to enforce the agreement and claim the royalties due to them.

K. R. Narayanan v. P. V. Rajam AIR 1997 Ker. 10:

Facts: The case of K. R. Narayanan v. P. V. Rajam was a copyright infringement case filed in the Kerala High Court. The Plaintiff, K. R. Narayanan, was the author of a Malayalam novel, "Amruthamanthram", and had registered the copyright for the same. The Defendant, P. V. Rajam, was the author of a novel titled "Amruthamanthram", which was allegedly an infringement of the Plaintiff's copyrighted work.

Issue: The main issue in the case was whether the Defendant's novel was an infringement of the Plaintiff's copyrighted work.

Judgment: The Kerala High Court found that the Defendant's novel was indeed an infringement of the Plaintiff's copyrighted work, and ordered the Defendant to pay damages to the Plaintiff. The Court noted that the Defendant had copied substantial portions of the Plaintiff's novel and had even used the same title, which was evidence of infringement. The Court also observed that since the Plaintiff had registered the copyright for his novel, it was prima facie evidence of originality and the Defendant had failed to prove that the novel was independently created. The court also observed that the defendant had not given any credit to the Plaintiff for the borrowed matter and it was a violation of the copyright act. The Court held that the Defendant was liable for copyright infringement and ordered him to pay damages to the Plaintiff.

Indian Music Industry v. Super Cassettes Industries Ltd. (SUPER CASSETTES) AIR 2007 Del. 8:

Facts:

The Indian Music Industry (IMI) filed a suit against Super Cassettes Industries Ltd. (SUPER CASSETTES) for copyright infringement.

IMI alleged that SUPER CASSETTES had been manufacturing, selling and distributing sound recordings of musical works without obtaining a license or permission from IMI, who held the copyright for the musical works in question.

SUPER CASSETTES argued that they had obtained a license from the Phonographic Performance Limited (PPL), a society for collection of royalties for sound recordings, and that this license covered their actions.

Issue:

The main issue in this case was whether or not SUPER CASSETTES had infringed on the copyright held by IMI by manufacturing, selling and distributing sound recordings of musical works without obtaining a license or permission from IMI.

Judgment:

The court held that SUPER CASSETTES had indeed infringed on the copyright held by IMI by manufacturing, selling and distributing sound recordings of musical works without obtaining a license or permission from IMI.

The court rejected SUPER CASSETTES' argument that they had obtained a license from PPL, stating that a license from PPL did not cover the manufacturing, selling and distributing of sound recordings, and that these activities required a separate license from the copyright holder.

The court ordered SUPER CASSETTES to pay damages to IMI and also to stop manufacturing, selling and distributing sound recordings of the musical works in question without a license or permission from IMI.

W.B. Yeats Ltd v. A.N. Naik (1992) 1 SCC 468:

Facts: The Plaintiff, W.B. Yeats Ltd, was the exclusive assignee of the copyrights of the literary works of W.B. Yeats, the famous Irish poet. The Defendant, A.N. Naik, published a book of poetry entitled "Golden Treasury of Indo-Anglican Poetry" which included several of Yeats' poems without obtaining permission from the Plaintiff or paying royalties.

Issue: The issue in this case was whether the Defendant's unauthorized publication of Yeats' poems in his book amounted to copyright infringement.

Judgement: The Supreme Court of India held that the Defendant's unauthorized publication of Yeats' poems in his book did constitute copyright infringement. The Court held that the Plaintiff had the exclusive right to reproduce, publish and sell Yeats' literary works, and that the Defendant's unauthorized use of these works without permission or payment of royalties amounted to a violation of these rights. The Court granted an injunction against the Defendant's future publication of Yeats' poems and ordered him to pay damages to the Plaintiff. The Court also held that the copyright of literary works is a property right that can be transferred and assigned to another person, and that the Plaintiff had validly obtained the exclusive rights to Yeats' works through assignment.

Marque Communications Inc. v. T.R. Rajagopalan AIR 1997 SC 3011:

Facts: Marque Communications Inc, a US-based company, filed a suit against T.R. Rajagopalan, a resident of India, for copyright infringement of its software program "Smart-1" which was used in the defendant's computer systems. Marque Communications Inc. claimed that the defendant had copied the software without obtaining any license or permission from the company.

Issue: Whether the defendant had infringed the copyright of Marque Communications Inc. by using its software without obtaining any license or permission.

Judgment: The Supreme Court held that the defendant had infringed the copyright of Marque Communications Inc. by using the software without obtaining any license or permission. The court held that copyright subsists in original literary, dramatic, musical and artistic works, including computer programs and any reproduction of such work without the permission of the copyright owner would amount to copyright infringement. The court also held that copyright subsists in original literary, dramatic, musical and artistic works, including computer programs and any reproduction of such work without the permission of the copyright owner would amount to copyright infringement. The court also held that the defendant's act of using the software without obtaining any license or permission amounted to copyright infringement and ordered the defendant to pay damages to the plaintiff.

Eastern Book Co v. D.B. Modak (2008) 5 SCC 1:

Facts: Eastern Book Company (EBC), a publisher of legal texts and commentaries, filed a suit against D.B. Modak, a retired judge of the Bombay High Court, for infringement of copyright in a judgment delivered by him while serving as a judge. EBC claimed that it had obtained the copyright in the judgment through assignment from the Registrar of the Bombay High Court and that Modak had reproduced substantial portions of the judgment in a book authored by him without obtaining EBC's permission.

Issue: The main issue in this case was whether the judgment delivered by a judge in a court of law can be considered as a literary work and therefore be eligible for copyright protection.

Judgment: The Supreme Court of India ruled that the judgment delivered by a judge in a court of law is a literary work and can be eligible for copyright protection. The Court held that the judgment is the product of the judge's intellect and effort and that it is not in the public domain merely because it is delivered in a court of law. The Court further held that the assignment of the copyright in the judgment by the Registrar of the Bombay High Court to EBC was valid and that Modak had infringed EBC's copyright by reproducing substantial portions of the judgment in his book without obtaining EBC's permission. The Court ordered Modak to pay damages to EBC and also to account for the profits he had made from the sale of the infringing book.

Indian Performing Right Society Ltd. v. Sanjay Dalia & Ors. (2015) SCC OnLine Del 8897:

Facts:

Indian Performing Right Society (IPRS) is an association of copyright owners of literary and musical works.

They filed a suit against Sanjay Dalia and others, who were operating a restaurant and a banquet hall, for infringement of their copyright by playing recorded music in their establishment without obtaining a license from IPRS.

Issue:

The main issue in this case is whether the defendants were guilty of copyright infringement by playing recorded music in their establishment without obtaining a license from IPRS.

Judgment:

The court held that playing recorded music in a commercial establishment without obtaining a license from the copyright owner or their authorized representative amounts to copyright infringement.

The court also held that the defendants were guilty of copyright infringement and ordered them to obtain a license from IPRS and pay a fine for the infringement.

The court also held that if the defendants continue to use the copyrighted music without obtaining a license, they will be liable to pay damages to the copyright owners.

Super Cassettes Industries Limited v. M/s. R.K. Films and Video (P) Ltd. (2000) 3 SCC 571

Facts: The case of Super Cassettes Industries Limited v. M/s. R.K. Films and Video (P) Ltd. (2000) 3 SCC 571 involved a dispute between Super Cassettes Industries Limited (the Plaintiff) and M/s. R.K. Films and Video (P) Ltd. (the Defendant) over the copyright infringement of a song. The Plaintiff, Super Cassettes Industries Limited, is a leading music company that holds the copyright to several songs and audio recordings. The Defendant, M/s. R.K. Films and Video (P) Ltd., is a film production company that had used a song owned by the Plaintiff in one of their films without obtaining permission.

Issue: The main issue in this case was whether the Defendant had infringed the Plaintiff's copyright by using the song in their film without obtaining permission.

Judgement: The Supreme Court of India held that the Defendant had infringed the Plaintiff's copyright by using the song in their film without obtaining permission. The Court noted that the Defendant had not obtained a license or permission from the Plaintiff to use the song and that the Plaintiff had the exclusive right to reproduce, distribute and communicate the song to the public. The Court also noted that the Defendant's unauthorized use of the song had resulted in financial loss to the Plaintiff and ordered the Defendant to pay damages to the Plaintiff. The court also held that the Defendant should have obtained the permission from the copyright holder before using the song in their film.

Najma Heptulla v. Orient Longman AIR 1989 Del 63

Facts: In this case, Najma Heptulla, a former Union Minister of India and a well-known author, had written a book titled "Islam: A Way of Life". The book was published by Orient Longman, a publishing company. The Defendant, Orient Longman, had published an abridged version of the book without the author's permission. The Plaintiff, Najma Heptulla, filed a suit for copyright infringement against the Defendant.

Issue: The main issue in this case was whether the Defendant, Orient Longman, had infringed on the Plaintiff's copyright by publishing an abridged version of the book without the author's permission.

Judgement: The Court held that the Defendant, Orient Longman, had indeed infringed on the Plaintiff's copyright by publishing an abridged version of the book without the author's permission. The Court granted an injunction restraining the Defendant from publishing or selling the abridged version of the book and also awarded damages to the Plaintiff. The court also held that the copyright owner has the right to control the reproduction of the work and to prevent others from producing copies of it without permission.

Additional Resources And Contact Information

"We at ISERD India are proud to have published "Guidebook on Indian Copyright Law for Creators and Users". We believe this book will serve as a valuable resource for those looking to understand and navigate the complexities of the Copyright Act, 1957.

As we come to the end of this book, we would like to remind our readers that the field of intellectual property law is constantly evolving, and new developments may occur after the publication of this book. We recommend that you check our website, www.iserdindia.com, for any updates or new information related to the Copyright Act, 1957 and other intellectual property laws.

We would also like to invite our readers to share their feedback and suggestions on how we can improve future editions of this book or other publications. You can reach out to us at contactus@iserdindia.com.

In addition, we would like to inform you that ISERD India provides training and consultancy services on various intellectual property laws and regulations. Our team of experts can provide you with the necessary guidance and support for your specific needs. For more information, please visit our website or contact us at contactus@iserdindia.com

We hope that this book will serve as a valuable resource for anyone interested in the field of intellectual property law, and we thank you for choosing ISERD India as your partner in learning."

9 798888 591924